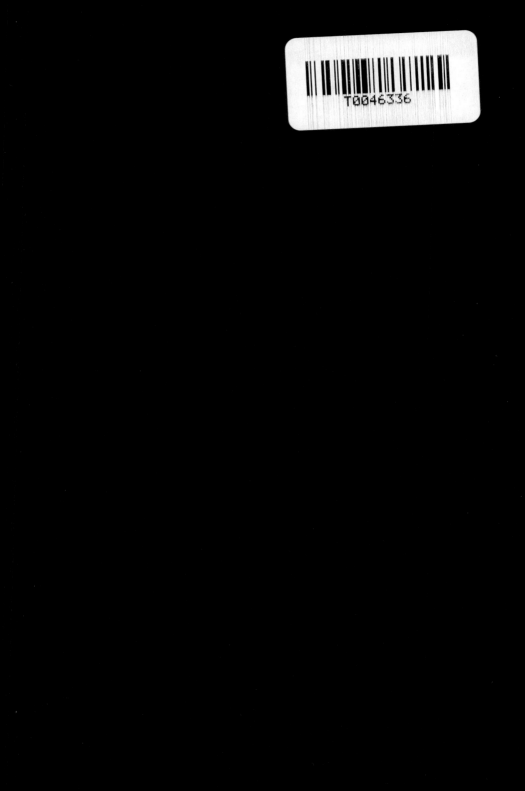

Trailer Park Shakes

Trailer Park Shakes

Justene Dion-Glowa

Brick Books

Library and Archives Canada Cataloguing in Publication

Title: Trailer park shakes / Justene Dion-Glowa.
Names: Dion-Glowa, Justene, author.
Identifiers: Canadiana (print) 20220266522 | Canadiana (ebook) 20220266530 |
ISBN 9781771315906 (softcover) | ISBN 9781771315913 (HTML) |
ISBN 9781771315920 (PDF)
Subjects: LCGFT: Poetry.
Classification: LCC PS8607.I6466 T73 2022 | DDC C811/.6—dc23

We gratefully acknowledge the Canada Council for the Arts, the Government of Canada
through the Canada Book Fund, and the Ontario Arts Council for their support of our
publishing program.

 Canada Council Conseil des arts
for the Arts du Canada Canadä ONTARIO ARTS COUNCIL
CONSEIL DES ARTS DE L'ONTARIO

Edited by Andrea Thompson and River Halen Guri.
Cover image by Kaija Heitland.
Author photo by Kali Smith, AllMemories Photography.
The book is set in Kepler.
Design by Marijke Friesen.
Printed and bound by Coach House Printing.

Brick Books
487 King St. W.
Kingston, ON
K7L 2X7
www.brickbooks.ca

Though much of the work of Brick Books takes place on the ancestral lands of the
Anishinaabeg, Haudenosaunee, Huron-Wendat, and Mississaugas of the Credit peoples,
our editors, authors, and readers from many backgrounds are situated from coast to coast
to coast in Canada on the traditional and unceded territories of over six hundred nations
who have cared for Turtle Island from time immemorial. While living and working on
these lands, we are committed to hearing and returning the rightful imaginative space
to the poetries, songs, and stories that have been untold, under-told, wrongly told, and
suppressed through colonization.

CONTENTS

I.

II.

For J, K, A, B, J, Z, D, M, J, J,
and all the youth they left behind.

I.

Tissue

The desire for specialness runs thick in my marrow –
a spider egg sac explosion waiting to
unload its writhing progeny onto this world.
A million ethereal arms reaching out in the darkness,
to be met by slapping hands and
balled-up tissue.

Greatness is a deep valley where
despair also lives.

I spit a web of vast proportions, hoping to finally
make
someone
stick.

blur

a twitch in your lower eyelid –
a constant nagging blur in your reality
barely perceptible to people around
you
you feel you must be seen
as a palpitating monster ready to lunge
and spread this infection
to anyone who'll let you
close enough to bite

Dust Bowl Masquerade

A fleeting moment of beauty in this husk of a town
Dust bowl – masquerade in lilac and peach

Squeeze feet into crystalline heels
kiss a prince & he'll forget me in the haze of booze & weed smoke
& family will still live to wreak havoc on another day
I can't decide if the mice are really singing
if the birds are helping design my gowns or if we're just

      high like when we

danced on broken glass all night

bloodied footprints leaving the ballroom

of a dying town //   //bleeding out

Fade to falling ashes & the swirling fury of storm
Watch the riverbed crack
Through plumes of smoke the mass migration hides its

     p a t   t e r   n

I'll migrate too
leave this place & live my life without the

tar on my back – steady eating away my flesh
burning and seeping

It doesn't hurt anymore
        Just

a dull ache like your heart gets
when you know it's over

Burial//Rebirth

i.) **Burial**

Mouth full of pebbles I can't
bear to spit out
They've been holding my tongue
    while
rolling around forcing a peace
between myself and the feeling
that
something ain't right

            That itch on
      your tongue
               that
           stomach full of
    cicadas –
      there's nothing for it

I've been trying to find a proper
description of their bouquet –
somewhere between coffee and
eucharist wine
the smell of heartbreak and regret
An earthy wooden finish
like a coffin
soil bound

My mouth full but still running
won't stop speaking ill of all the
ills

Can't not be candid with your
mouth full

ii.) **Rebirth**

Pebbles turn to manna from
heaven; falling

into the screeching mouths of
baby birds –
maws waiting

Slip silent into the nest little dove
Strip the branches
Make the wood bare

Make the others yearn for your
song
Have the mommas wail your tune
Hit your notes and dive deep
Catch the breeze last minute
Make my heart skip its beats

7

kaanookaat

{spider}

Hello tiny friend
You are mildly creepy but harmless
You tap tap your spinneret
expanding your bathtub-long empire
You have knees that knurl
with bulges defining the limbs
Your web is near invisible
but it bends in the middle
And that's where I can see you best

What does it feel like to wield power over such a great creature as
    humankind?
To inspire fear at the top of the food chain?
How can I take that power for my own?
Tap tap my spinneret
Build an invisible empire
only the naked and vulnerable will find
Too afraid to squash me
Too afraid to let me live
Maybe catch me in a little cup and throw me outside
to rebuild a larger kingdom
To feast
To thrive

Thistle&Thorn

Redemption's curled up catlike on a path tangled over with thistle
    and thorn

Jutting brambles a reminder of a lack of
{{warmth and depth}}
that have led to this nettle imbroglio
If the cuts get you deeply then you're failing as a woman
If the cuts leave scars then you're triumphant in recovery
But there's simply no way there will not be cuts
We will not inherit our thrones
We will build them
Perhaps first from thistle and thorn and then
later
                from gold and ether

We will sit upon them –

                        Monsters

ruts

going fast as I please

I light sage in hope
the Devils won't find me
but the ruts keep me from

they gonna catch up
follow the ashes I burnt away
the trail of little matchsticks
I used to call a home

compass spins and whirls
it wont help me find the way
it's just pointing to where my
heart feels best

in the ruts there are dead birds
at least one each day
their feathers sing
standing in the wind

but they still in the gutter.

Ghost

A manic-punk-kid-disillusioned-adult-fuck-a-plan rebellion
speaks to something in my dark little sleep-with-the-drummer
soul, maybe because he was a good lay but also maybe because he
was actually someone I really loved. So I razed all the cities I had
ever known, burned every bridge I crossed to wipe the memory
clean of this person {read: me} I thought I knew – when the bridge
fell the water rippled like TV static – a smoothly meandering
wave pattern hoping not to pick up a haunt à la *Poltergeist*. But it
did. My ghost stuck around because no matter how much chaos
I ignited it wouldn't take away the absolute shit I made people
go through just to get close to me. The guilt, in other words. But
eventually they saw right through me – I was just a spectre of a
person they once knew, likely a fraud and almost certainly a pain
in the ass to get rid of. Turn that static up a little louder and let me
hear it play its song so that maybe…

Maybe

I can reach someone who gives a shit again.

Sertraline Dreams

Level 1

I'm in a video game. It's virtual reality and it's confusing to say the least, a game I've never played before.

There are shiny golden rings to collect and they lead you where the game wishes you to go.

At some point I realize I am the villain.

I am the monster people are running from.

But the game is still fun.

My body writhes along with other bodies against the walls of a darkened brick and mortar chamber.

As I climax I realize this is perverse and disgusting and I fuck monsters now.

Level 2

I am climbing the walls of a dungeon. I am evil incarnate. I destroy everything I touch. The bloodlust rises in my belly.

I keep quiet to follow my prey.

Cut Scene:

I have kidnapped a perfectly normal human. I am drowning him in cement. I am flying into the night carrying his carcass in my talons. Fade to black.

Level 3

In this game everyone is disfigured either literally or metaphorically. Monstrous on the outside with a heart of gold, or

beautiful exteriors with empty eyes. I do not know which category
I belong in.

Level 4
I am lucid enough to wonder:
how many milligrams of this drug does it take to feel calm again?
My shrink says I'm on a pretty low dose but
I want off the ride.

When it slips past my senses and slices right into the fibre of me –

Where do I feel that? I don't even know. Does it change who I am?
Do I lose a tiny piece of myself like the flashing hearts in the
corner of the screen every time I down the cure?
Why do I feel guilty? It's only a dream…

Level 6
Serenity is overrated. Chaos is God.

Level 7
I have died. I hope I don't have to start over at the beginning again.

Level 1
No checkpoints.
Full hearts.
Little power.
Medium stamina.
I'm still the monster people are running from.

But I am not scared.

I collect the shiny golden rings and watch the numbers count up on the screen.

My depression, my husband, and me

Don't worry about it. I will be fine. I am always fine because I trim the kids' nails and make sure they eat thrice daily and I've ordered their school pictures also when I get home the dishwasher better be empty I think I've done it the last three times but oh thank you so much for all your help. Please, please let me know if there is anything I can do for you before you walk out into the darkness never to return. Hey have you seen that receipt before you go? It's really important. Omg fuck now I have to pull over Babe did you want me to come get you? The new house is super loud right now with the renos but I bet you won't hear it over the sounds of your internal screaming. How can I help? I went shopping today I got a bunch of food Babe if you need anything call me in an hour, no half an hour. Should I take them all? Take them all at once? An hour is long enough to digest. Kids what can I make you for lunch? When will they notice? When will they see it? Why don't they help? Can't they see it? I am almost dying from it but here they are just smiling. Is the darkness gone? I'm so proud of you. Do you have anyone else you can call to talk to right now? Do you have a friend you could call? Why can't I say anything without you laughing? Tell me how to feel. It's better that way. You know I'm so proud of everything you've done these last few weeks. You made it there you didn't even pull over. I told you to help me to please help me and you made it to your destination without even stopping or turning around. Is this a joke to you? Is it okay with you that I want to off myself at least once a week? Sure blame me, everyone else does. You know what if we just have sex we will both be able to sleep better because omg I barely slept again last night. Are you

there? Are you there? Are you there? Are you there? Are you there?
Are you there?

A   RE   YO   U   TH

                                                        E

                                         R

                                E

                          ?

Shakes

The trailer park shakes when the trains go by
I can't tell yet if it's a comfort or a curse but
I always loved the sound of trains in the distance.

You can hear every word of conversation going on next door
And the other neighbours don't like weed smoke.

The heater grinds. It's so loud it could tear the roof off
But we've got a washer and dryer so I don't have to go to the
laundromat anymore.

There's a skylight in the kitchen where sunlight dances onto the
floor and dazzles the kids who come over
and the stars twinkle in our eyes when the nights are clear.

Our fence is broken. Pretty badly. Same with the deck. And the stairs
But the view from here is spectacular
The river and the mountains
And the trains that shake the house.

In the back is a mountainside
The desert type
Very sandy soil though there are a lot of pines up that way. A lot of
sage too
My cat plays out there
He is quite the hunter so we don't get a lot of mice in the house
anymore

There're some garden beds out back too
Maybe we'll plant in the spring.

My bedroom is quite big now
It's nice to have a big space to call your own
Usually I give the kids the biggest room to share
But not this time.

I wonder if the kids know they're poor
I wonder if it has dawned on them just yet
I don't think it has
I don't think they know how close they live to ruin
I never did.

That's what a good parent is
Able to hide the worst of the situation
and bring out the best

You don't have to be rich to have a good life but it helps I guess.

I don't remember feeling poor
But I remember my dad working 3 jobs
And I remember the day I realized that even though I thought all it
took was hard work to get ahead in life
it actually takes a garbage bag of weed and a lot of clients
and after 20 years
you'll still be in the shit.

But they don't tell you that.

And it's hard to remember when you get older
that no one ever really did it on the level anyway
That everything you thought you knew
about how to be an effective adult is just misinformation
That it really is just one fucked up situation after another in a
never-ending loop.
But that doesn't mean the world is out to get you
It just means that's all the world has to offer at this time.

Frankly it's not surprising that no matter how steady I start to feel
the train still makes the whole house shake.

My dad used to tell me that the sound of the trains used to make
him cry
but he didn't know why
Maybe intergenerational trauma got him
the way it gets all us imperfect simpletons
just trying to make it to next pay day.

When the trailer park shakes I wonder
if my mother had a trailer that shook
too
I wonder why we always end up going full circle
I wonder how it is that no matter how hard we have worked we
never really make it
I wonder how at 14 she managed to raise a kid
And how 11 months later she had 2 to take care of
How she stuck by this man who knocked up a child
and had the audacity to call her wife

I wonder how she went to school and worked and fed us
Then I realize why I don't need to wonder why she fucked up
so badly
none of us talk to her anymore

And one of us is already dead.

My trailer isn't much
But it's these people who make it a home
Cuz a house is just a box
Kind of like a body is for the soul.

sunday best

on the weekends we would go the kingdom hall
mom ready to receive the word of god and my heart ready to
doubt every syllable

only had the one nice dress so wore it every time
to every wedding and special occasion that occurred while it still fit
an awful floral print of mostly green with hints of purple
foreshadowing the bruises left by landline phones tossed in my
    direction
when the booze became the light jehovah was s'posed to be
the crinoline itched mercilessly
so unlike that godly benevolence I just couldn't seem to feel

I sort of had a friend there
but we all know that ended where my questions began
I wondered what to think when they said we shouldn't see people
outside the faith
how that included so many people I loved
how that would come to include me
in my sunday best
too poor to wear another dress
and too unfaithful to have god provide another

Breadline

The food bank makes you show ID
for you and your kids and anyone else in the house
so you don't get too much

They'll give you more if you're pregnant tho

At the food bank a person stands behind each section of the tables to
make sure you only take
what you're allowed
Once I got a whole bag of potatoes but
my kids don't eat those

And hemp milk is horrible

I would bus all over town to get to all the food banks
that were open on different days
so we could actually eat
cuz one never gives you enough for the week

I got sick from the leftovers once cuz
I didn't have anything to wrap em up in

At the food bank you act like this is all normal and everything is okay
so the kids don't know they're about to starve

You dress them in free clothes from your auntie

And read them books the library discarded

It reminds you that
your grandma kept her food stamps from the great depression
and was obsessed with overstocking the house with food

The food banks are all at churches
and you wonder why there's no place to get this
in a secular type of way

I'd sell my soul to the devil
to make sure these kids eat

traces

they didn\t tell me \til she\d died
   what she\d done
what she\d done couldn\t really be called incest
\cause that might mean maybe they both wanted to

but you   can\t want to when someone is
in an authoritative role

      say like your ██ or something

you can\t want to when

they are   older than you

you cAN\T want to when

they know it\s wrong because they have sons they\d never want that
done to
but you\re young & afraid
& can\t want to when you\re too scared to know

that women do rape
& men   can be

when you don\t wanna say \cause you don\t want it to be real
you can\t want to & it won\t heal you

to know she is dead
to know she got rid of herself
maybe \cause   the guilt
maybe \cause   the pain
it won/t heal you
to know her secrets didn\t go to her grave

dust devils stirred up \cause death made them safe

maybe her ashes blew away in that storm
          just meaningless filth
      skimming the wind

or maybe now

the ashes have drawings in them
of a little stick boy
too hurt & scared to say
& a lot of adults standing \round him
too afraid to be right

The Norm

He was just small,
beaten so badly they buried his clothing in the backyard to hide
    the blood
so he wouldn't get taken away.

In jail since I can remember.
The gift he received on his 18th birthday was to be moved from
juvenile detention to minimum security.
He graduated to max later.
Taught me how to play solitaire on our visits.
Tried to teach me chess when I got older.

I was pregnant the first time they asked to strip search me. It was
    smut.

I still can't play chess.

My aunt told me over family dinner that she had seen my brother
on the 10 most wanted.
Never realized how cruel that was until I was much older.

He came to our brother's funeral in shackles with two plain-
clothes guards.
I held his cuffed hand, gaped at his chained ankles.

They let him wear some decent clothes at least.

Much later, he criticized my eulogy for our brother.

It was a packed house even though half of them knew they'd be arrested at the end of the service.

So thank you for accepting that risk, I guess.

And they were. Squad cars packed to overflowing with the kids I grew up with.

Fully grown but somehow

not quite.

Invitation

They invited me to go see his dead body
in that sterilized room with that
smell of CaviCide
those white coats and
white sheets

Them black bags
zipper like a Y-incision
the one that desecrates his chest
made to help the policy man decide
if he could save some money
even if it meant starving some kids

The editor asked me
would I comment one year later
after they threw his name up in their papers
A gangster that somehow never

caught a charge

Just another sprinkling of salt in the wounds of his children
who definitely get that paper every day

Unsubscribe

Now the kids barely remember his name
but their wounds loom large enough to see through
– person shaped –
the healing that got done washed away
by another moment he won't share
nothing but a namesake
for a little boy
he'll never
meet

One son, white as snow, likes to shoot off guns for fun
One blue-eyed, dark-skinned boy, who always promises to stay
clean another day
And a blonde girl who can hardly muster the memory of his face
before the life left it

None of them got the invitation –
'cept to see Daddy carried out on a stretcher

Meadowood Daze

In the Meadowood
we skip along
Just children
playing at being grown

   at knowing something

We don't have the wherewithal
to get behind one another
prop each other up

         We attack
         We scheme
         We don't know what it means

We speak in riddles like that's how it works
We talk shit behind each other's backs
But stay friends just the same
It's easier to believe in one another
   than it is to believe someone will   intervene

      Inexplicably

we all end up fine
We all end up in the   hereafter

The Van Man

The van man stops us right out back
in the alley behind Claudette's
She is the brave one
I am small and scared

I don't know if we ever told anyone except
Claudette's mom
She only seemed mildly concerned but
with six daughters what hadn't she heard?

The van man invites us in
asks if we want a ride

Claudette says no
I do not speak
The van man asks again
Claudette runs
I follow
I wonder how she knew
I wonder if I had been alone
I wonder often about things that
never came to fruition
Even now that I'm older
And now that I know what the van man wants
I wonder if there are Claudettes out there

saving little girls
one at a time

II.

Archive

Plucked
The dermis all goose flesh in texture
Anticipating
daylight that will never arrive

The damp hits
dry sweetgrass
Sweat
on the corpse of a plant

Buzz
Baby flies with butts all fuzzy blue
sweep the scene
for signs of life

But the tears on disappointed cheeks
of little boys
don't dry
They entomb

Din

Moonglow shakes the birch as I walk
serenely to the altar

She awaits a sacrifice from the womb

I have given much to this altar
but
my efforts have been fruitless even
if multiplied

Summer virgins sing in the copse of trees
their voices a ghostly wail riding the air
A psalm for the long dead and still dying

The trees watch
glint on blade
careen downward
to the stone
where once I sat

Where once I was seen
A scarlet melody bursts its banks
An arrhythmic refrain
for the dead and me

wick

all the nails bitten down to the quick –

the under-skin   raw and exposed   has a sheen to it
blood never bothered to help heal the wound

will your scattered bare bones still feel the ache of a long day upright
or
does the chill of that encroaching inky blackness ice the injury
?

      you will leave your stain on the everyday
        when you trip over oblivion's edge
//

there is no turning back

this agreement is written in blood it's indelible like the mark we
leave on loved ones   it's tattooed in the air that hovers above
your corpse like a ghost

it smells of sulfur

too many matchsticks burnt down to the fingers that hold them –

their flesh is your flesh   breathe it in before you quit breathing

light the wick before the darkness hurts

you are ending

this only ceases when you cease to exist so keep running til your

lungs ache the way embers ache for whirlwinds

the water is still
the air is mute
the grasses rest
the fire cleansed

Perch

I want that steadiness on my feet

To always land right side
up
Make the leap
with such dexterity
Bear witness to the world

Ever present//all knowing

Destroyer of worlds and
keeper of none

Will you notice when I
carry the fire for you
Bring an end to all that's happened
then fly into the
realm of angels

Halo firmly perched

For my god knows no masters
'cept for the knowledge

of

my kin and me

kornay

{crow}

Black feathers in the wind
wave anarchy then death

Friends gather and cry out
A tumultuous resting place
on a backroad centre line

I pick that raven up
Its blood runs furrows in the creases of my skin
drips a dotted line to where x marks a final spot

No gravestone

Just a brown paper towel from my glovebox to give closure
to a murder of crows weeping at the crime scene
A congress that bears witness to the killing
while I hope the neighbours don't see

shoovreu
{deer}

Your eyes are black
not unlike my own
filled with transcendental dread
and knowing
all the horrors of this world before the blackness hit

I wonder if your
tongue lolled
out
but I missed it in my hurried passing

What is it like to see calamity coming?

I don't want to die with my eyes open

THE DARK PLACE

Stop   I said
He did but his hands still lingered on my body – not sure what
level of stop this was
and
he needed to be asked again
Stop   I said

I'm in the dark place

Not so much a memory as an inkling
A sensation that something is not right and may never be
I tell myself this is part of the process
This is how we heal and
this is why it feels so fresh

I tell him
        I don't know why I go to the dark place
        I don't know where it is
        And I don't know who first took me there but
        I can't ignore it
sneaking up on me like –

In legions of bodily millimetres there might be one that
        cannot contain its fury when grazed upon

He says he understands and truly
he shows he does

If only hands leaving body meant psyche back to present
skin scorched from a memory too charred to really see

Surely it is no coincidence that
violation and immolation
contain
the same number of syllables

Hark! A Misandrist!

Misandry! he cries.

I shake my head not wanting to upset the men who I fear could be a danger to me. I tell him when I was young I learned to be nice so men didn't harm me. No men speak at that.

Hark! A Misandrist!

Well surely she must be, to reject the advances of someone like you, is that what you mean? There's no chance that it's you who's the problem? Not you who needs a "mis" type word to describe your tone?

Extra Extra! Misandry Abounds!

Here we are discussing sex like it's money. Like the poor need a handout. Like that's not one of the most problematic things ever uttered in the pages of a highly respected mainstream publication.

Hark! A survivor!

Some man will be around shortly to tell you you're exploiting #MeToo and that all you want is attention while he slowly backs you into a corner and you, likely still fearful, remain kind. Save the anger for a safer time. Doesn't really matter which man does it? Because #NotAllMen so it's fine.

Hark! An Incel!

If only we permitted men to use us as they please perhaps they would stop murdering us in the streets – but those streets lead to homes, where women are murdered by men who "love" them.

Hark! A Lion!

Is it me or him? Will I be the one to roar my rage while the predator closes in? While the police decide what care to give based on the pigment in skin? And when we bring the fight back to the whole pride, it's still on us. Still our clothes and our makeup and our colour and our living and our breathing that decide exactly who's to blame.

Hark! A Misogynist!

Did you need me to define that for you? Need me to help explain it to you so you can explain it back to me? Did me calling you out make you feel bad oh no let me tend to that emotional labour for you while I spiral downward and you watch without seeing, witness without grieving –

Hark! A Feminist!

We're all man haters here. Now your job is to convince us why we shouldn't be.

CRUSH(ED)

That feeling on the bus when you sit across from the girl with the side shave and the longboard with her purple sparkly perfectly-trimmed-for-fucking fingernails screaming gay at you but you'll never get the courage to scream it back

The knowledge that in queer spaces with queer people you always have to come up with some way to explain the straight partner and phrase your queerness just so, juxtaposing the privilege of passing as straight with your gratitude for inclusion in the LGBT

Your panged chest when you catch the eye of the extra butch lesbian at pride but goddamn if she ain't already with someone who looks exactly like you right down to the tattoos – oh if only you could fuck a girl once in a while

The weight of your partner letting you know that at any time if you just need to take off and grab a hotel room and spend some of your time sexing up women as though there would be no guilt or feelings associated with that

Your heart knowing you are not polyamorous but if only you could be for a little while and actually experience what it's like to love and be loved by a woman, not that I'm saying polyamorous folks have it easy

Your spirit knowing that at least once a year you will have to justify yourself to others in a vain attempt to assure them that yes, you are in fact as bi as they come

Your being when you do not fit inside this godforsaken box everyone insists on putting you in –

No I will not pick a side

Yes I am happy with my husband

Yes I am simultaneously occasionally sad there isn't a beautiful woman in my heart and in my bed

No you might not get what it's like but – I know someone out there has felt this deep in their bones and I think maybe

the girl on the bus with the side shave and the longboard with her purple sparkly perfectly-trimmed-for-fucking fingernails probably understands, too

she

bedroom eyes glitter like zirconia

full of serotonin & dopamine

clustered

together

the soft sway of plush bodies

against each other

against the world

lips press & tongues shudder

fingertips graze quivering bareness

rhythm   actualized in form

warmth of exhalation

a pausing apogee

she moves

she breathes

she is

just a dream

Aces

A perfume bottle for a booze can
Found out what rape was by 4 and
by 6 had a porn habit from the misunderstanding
I cried to Mom and Dad about it
in the middle of the night
wracked by guilt over
some shit that's not my fault
Or a fault at all

CFS should've taken me when they had the chance to

help   but

we know they make things worse

Once Mom brought me over to a crack house and left me there
But the folks there were nice enough
I saw one of the guys from that house later in a different town
Said he had never forgotten me

{Grandad stuck a 45 in his daughter's mouth and so
this life is the legacy}

I was scared when mom would drink
And my neighbour was nice til he stalked me
But I took the roses he left outside anyway
cuz I didn't really know
what *no* was

Like the man who tried to coerce my 15-year-old self to come try
doggy style at his house
The penetration is just so deep he said
But that day I got let go
/virginity/ intact
instead of waking up with fingers inside me
while the porno played
Like that other time

The 20-year-old I dated at 16
who I guess figured there was no power structure there
who wouldn't acknowledge me in public
but who I still can't really say the word rape about
even after someone said it for me

Or the cheap feels in the pit at a metal show but
I'm the one who left the scene

Yes means yes not
no means no because
no is a powerful word for someone who
wields none

I wonder why I'm triggered by things I shouldn't be and then I
realize
I shouldn't wonder

I would run without even knowing where is safe
What safe is as a concept

More than once just the crack of light beneath the basement door
for company
The knob would never turn on those days

Once I visited Grandma and I pined over one of her lipstick shades
while she drank perfume
She told us Grandad came back and raped her and
they
told her she was bipolar

So I learned

Cute kids can't cure

And

we
don't
learn
lessons
til we
learn em

the
hard
way

Vessel

I walk right by those cans you don't even have the decency to empty
as my head thrums a disjointed chorus
Memories of what you've said to me
wound my already weakened heart

I see those cans tucked everywhere
from the shower to the car and laundry room
When I tell you I think you felt better without the booze
you stay silent for a while –

then pick a fight about some unrelated things

When I get so panicked I must act
I will put those cans in a trash bag
just to be sure you don't get
any more money for the habit from the returns

Those cans remind me
I'm just a vessel for your dreams
a place to store what needs fulfilling

what you're too cowardly to admit you can't do on your own –

{{What I want becomes unspeakable
in the presence of your shame}}

The vessel is broken
But the stash just keeps getting thrown in
When the cracks can't hold together any longer
you'll scream you don't know how it broke

labour pains

how exactly does one explain emotional labour?
is it the twisting and turning of conflicting interests pulling your
marionette strings taut?
is it the weight of all the tears cried at you?
how does one say it?
how does one get it just right?
lord I'd hate to miss that mark

how do you express that the emotions of the grand Other have
swallowed your inner being and all that's left is a black hole

even that will soon be gone

surely there is a non-English word for this

how do you tell someone you love that you are spent on their
specific brand of bullshit?
what do you tell them to ease that scorch?
I certainly don't know   I've tried a lot of things
last night I pictured myself hanging from the rafters of the
basement and I figured this morning would be a pretty good time
to get that little plan going but

my apologies I've spent far too long talking about me
so do tell –

what does it take to have someone truly understand
to empathize even
with the idea that the burden you bear is so heavy
that your feet hurt so much you can barely walk but you'll still
walk your kids to school every day

when I breathe they hear it
but when I scream it comes out silent
I'm already crawling toward entropy   it's a burden to cross that
finish line I figure so why not embrace it?

    embrace your self care

I wish I could describe it but
all I can say is

it's a labour of love

SMS

My love

I'm sorry

My love I know u know I'm trying my best not just
trying I'm doing

My love I want to be there for you but I can't do
both I feel guilt but I have to make this right
to be there more for you

My love we are about a week away

My love we are close

My love it's almost time

My love

Xo

Scaffold

It takes partnership
to build it
A sturdy thing made to provide

        safety

          A net

              Something solid on
        which

                    to work
        But the rungs hurt on the come-down

        Each one a new wound

                   piercing
           bruising and breaking

         Your bones creak under the
      weight of you
      Just you

And the force you hit the ground with when you've fallen

     all the way

d

o

w

n

.

Business as Usual

I wish I could get behind your goals but
instead I am under them
In panic I dug a grave
like an animal clawing its way to refuge
not realizing the deeper I got the more trapped I became

You never visit the grave either –
there are no flowers here to remember me by
Just the crunch of dirt beneath my nails
as I scrape around for oxygen

I won't get any though
oxygen isn't very profitable
Nor is rest
Or peace
Acknowledgement is also bad for business
so we can't offer that today

But we do have a nice severance package for you
It comes complete with
the demise of your marriage
and maybe everything you once held dear
Who knows!
The possibilities are truly endless
Our design is one of a kind

I am still waiting for you to find where I am buried
but when you look you don't see me
You just see a perfect place to fit more of your dreams
and the weight is pushing me
further down than I ever wanted to go

Mixed Signals

Every time someone erases my queerness because of the kids or
the person I share a home with
I'm hollowed out –
a jack-o-lantern wearing a face someone else carved.
Too straight to be queer and too bi to be straight.

To survive this I imagine I'm a superhero.
I live a double life and I maintain it to keep those I love in relative
obscurity from enemies,
though I don't seem to know mine are real.

When I choke on the words I wish I could say but don't feel
entitled to, *Remember, you are powerful.*

When I pine after beautiful women but cannot utter a sound,
Remember, your secret keeps you safe.

Is my struggle less than that of others?
Is my pain less than that of others?
Is my hardship less than that of others?

That is to say –

is my queerness less than that of others?

The question wants to hollow me out

but

it does not have to be my truth.

Protégé Concubine

Boy poets – so conventionally "attractive"
with symmetrical good looks and just the right amount of stubble

Wearing ascots unironically
They struggle with mental health too you know
It has been hard for them
Oh so hard
Let's snap our fingers at Daddy a little louder
Daddy we totally buy your pain
Boy poets –

So cynical!
So devious!
So real!
Wow that boy can really make us feel!
Boy poets

Bound to this earthly realm to correct us and
neglect us and
show us how this is really done
Boy poets

Please give us all the advice you hope we need
Please
tell us again how love is so hard and
again how life is just hurt
Boy poets
Please don't harm us

Boy poets
Don't shame us
Boy poets
Lift us up like you lift your cock in dick pics
Boy poets

Blowing off steam into the progress of our careers
Telling us how women hurt them
Promising they're the ticket to getting published
Telling us every piece we write is amazing
No editing needed
As long as we
let them send it to their industry connections for us

Their little
protégé concubine

They discovered us and don't you forget it
They'll take us on tour but only far away where
we won't find escape from
Boy poets

#HotTake

My hot take is that no one can tell if you've been crying
if you exit the shower bleary eyed and splotched with red
It may even take them a while to find your corpse if you should
slip and fall
accidentally
You may romanticize those hard water crusts and mildew-
blackened corners all you wish –
you will still be nothing but poor poor poor

The rusted chain on the drain plug is a symbol of your plight
Forever shackled to a man and home that will never
Be enough

But you can be

And when you finally are
the question will hang in the air like a spectre
Is it okay?
Is it okay for me to be more
Do more
Have more
Earn more

Are we faking it but not making it?
Is it make and break?
Are these different things?

I been begging so long but
on my knees I'm just a whore and
upright I'm a fucking virago so –

My hot take is that if nothing changes, nothing changes
Whether you believe you can or you can't

you're right

The Slow Creeping Feeling That Everything Will Not Be Okay

Dissent –
somehow difficult to muster the inertia or gravitas to pull it off
The world is in slumber
This machine makes fascists
Rebellion quelled by the almighty dollar

I'm too busy – I gotta go to work
I got a family to feed
By the end of the day I'm too exhausted to even want to
hold a conversation or get laid

Rain all January
Fires all July
The revolution has been televised for nearly the last 50 years but
we change the fucking channel –
desperate for escape but
too despondent to even pack a bag
Can't afford to leave this town anyway
save a miracle that will only turn to a curse –

the grass does not get greener
the water all dried up

We unionize to save our spirits but
capitalize to quell our hunger
What difference does it make anyway if

we make a buck or give it away?
It's the same cycle – we are

disposable

//we are//

trapped

//we are//

mutiny

Roaring like a lion

watching videos of

kittens

The Gambler

Red eyed.
We're twins that way!
Me, from tears I've cried over your missing body.
You, the booze that makes the buttons easier for you to push.
How exciting to be sharing this dark time of our lives,
lit only by the twinkling lights and shrill buzz denoting a winner.
Yes, a special time to look back upon in earnest –
as though our struggle legitimized our love.

Plans made in secret
to escape the monster that took over your body instead of hiding in
its usual spot
in the corner of the room.
A screaming match and a smashed fist later, and we're lucky –
lucky we have each other …

aren't we?

With a stroller and a kindergartener I march to war
ready to do anything to pull you out of that abyss –
only to find the car missing. And my bank card. And my rent money.

An escape.
A trauma.
A deadline,
an overdraft,
and an idea that love is enough to live on.

But no.

These kids can't eat your efforts to change.
They cannot be clothed in broken promises.
They cannot live inside the hope I have that you will get better.

The stigma hits me like a ton of bricks – no one will take this
addiction seriously.
It's not a drug.
So
just stop.
Your struggle means nothing in the eyes of the world.
But we struggle on. On to those flashing lights and celebratory
bells at the end of the tunnel.

Well, you're the gambler. You tell me.

Is it worth the risk?

That Snapchat Filter Makes Me Look Like a Dead Man

You know the one
The one that makes you look full of machismo
and maybe steroids (the horse kind)
The one that gives you chin stubble and a slick fade
Square jawline for days
Thick eyebrows on fleek

I look alive
I look like my brother

7 grams

How many grams of crack in one's stomach is too much for the
coroner to rule the overdose accidental?
Or rather
what is the threshold for this particular insurance provider?
How many minutes did it take for his wife to decide it was time to
pull the pin
rather than care for my big brother the rest of his life?
A vegetable, the doctor called him –
you have to wonder if he was just another brown boy in that
doctor's eyes.
How long did it take for the ambulance to arrive
while the kids hid away or bore witness?
I think the bill must've been somewhere between four and eight
hundred.
Adding invoice to injury.
How long did it take for us to find the notes he left again?
I honestly can't remember.
It's likely better that I don't.
I write those notes myself from time to time.

And where is the rest of him I wonder,
looking at a vaguely familiar corpse of a man
I avoided so long, wearing the clothes of my brother –
his chains,
his shoes.

If I picture him with his eyes open he still looks dead,
only if I look long enough I will see him silently, subtly
mouthing a prayer to whatever god will take him in such a sorry
state.

How long did his dog stay lonely?
How long did his body stay cold before the flames warmed it –
gently at first,
then hot enough to transform it to powder,
bagged up and vacuum sealed,
stashed in a box.

Do they take the crack out of your stomach when they cut you
open?
How about the sleeping pills?
Do they have to count how many there are or do they just take
photos?
How many stitches did it take to close his chest?
How many years will it take to heal this wound?

That Boy

When That Boy spit sour in my Slurpee –
the one I rode all the way to Sev for –
I cursed him
I cursed him harder when he took my diary around town for an
impromptu spoken word tour

When That Boy came home, crawling out of his friend's Camaro
after four cops took turns beating him since
we all know natives don't own nice cars
Mom said *We'll take them to court* when she'd finished crying
the way only blonde-haired blue-eyed ladies do
Didn't see her son's brown skin and eyes
Just saw
her son
And That Boy deserved better

When That Boy came home from court and them cops got away
with it
Time off with pay is vacation not
retribution
Mom didn't understand it was
just the beginning of a long line of
shit to go wrong

When That Boy kept six for the ones called 'friends'
But never did any actual crime

That Boy took me to see my first ever tattoo get done
I saw what pain was but beauty too
and the kinda place I'd
never
wanna get tattooed in

When That Boy had me watch his kids
while he took his girl out to eat and drink
he came home and took her to the bathroom to beat her up over
some jealousy shit
I covered those kids' ears so
they couldn't hear their mother crying

When That Boy told me *No* –
Mom's buying booze not coffee
then showed me the half full tin as receipt
Said *No one takes a backpack grocery shopping*
then taught me the way to his place a little ways down the road

When That Boy showed me where he worked out
trying to make sure I was strong enough to handle what he
must've known
was coming

When That Boy lost weight I told him he looked skinny and he
scoffed
Fuck You
So I knew he quit the 'roids at least

When That Boy left home in an ambulance wail
he took the person I was then with him

The One & Only

The only picture I have of my oldest brother is from inside prison –
in the weight room, shirtless, puff chested, probably trying to look
hard for some girl he was seeing at the time.
But I figure, you only get to take so many photos while incarcerated,
so I got the double he took for someone else I guess.

It's from after his tattoo got dated.
I wonder how that went down for him in there.
        Everyone knowing
he was on the outs with folks who ran a lot of shit.

There's a bright yellow poster behind him with words etched in
sharpie:

> *ShoW Some Respect!*
> *Put weights away*
> *—paper towel*
> *—use garbage*

It's hard to read all the words with him standing in the way.

One time I tried to sneak in new shoes for him –
a man who'd been inside as long as he was old enough to face
charges.

I didn't think it was a big deal
      til they tried to strip search me before the visit.
      Obviously they'd listened to our phone call beforehand but

shoes is not code for anything.

      It's just shoes.

I never got to visit him again after that, no matter how many
appeals I made.
You can't blame them.
      {We all get trapped in the confines of
      bureaucracy from time to time}
But I still do.

n8v aunties

everything smells of sage at your native auntie's place

cat circles at your feet while she tells you stories of Sundance
makes a feast of KD and tomato soup so you get those veggies in
shows you how to tie tobacco
says *you gotta buy it now tho we all do, but get it in a pouch*

she tries to teach you how to bead but at that age it doesn't stick
later you'll wish you'd listened
to any damn thing

spiders crawl at your native auntie's
where it becomes painfully apparent you have not yet felt the song
pour from your hands to douse a drum
where the rattle lies still cuz there was no one to teach you how to
shake it – even your auntie doesn't know that

you learn so much but know so little
where the cedar hangs above every door
evergreen
where the renovations are always half done
where the carpet has spots that'll never come out
where you learn you can curl your native hair with a lot of bobby
pins
but it kinda comes out all crimpy from the bumps

at your native auntie's you might accidentally walk into the
neighbours' house cause the houses all look the same from the
front –
no one will say a word though
it's no big deal around here

you and your cousins stay up late
crouched under blankets on the floor
and the grown-ups cover your eyes when the movie gets too scary
and you steal from your older cousin only to
toss it back into her bag when she isn't looking

where every piece of fabric smells like dust
and there are blankets everywhere
and towels are few and far between

there's a mall by your native auntie's that seems so big
even though you know now what a dive it was

antlers hang at your native auntie's
you can put damn near anything in that freezer – it's always got
enough room for a hunt
she'll show you pictures of the last moose they cleaned
she'll warn you it's gory

at your native auntie's the backyard is small but full of toys for kids
that are too young to be her own

she takes you to yard sales so she can fill her kitchen with kitsch
she somehow always manages to pull off
everything is stacked against the walls at your native auntie's
there are books on top of books, but
one thing about being at your native auntie's is
it's always so comfortable no matter how full or cramped or
cluttered
and she sure makes your white aunty seem like a sterile bitch

your native auntie is always ready to tell you to leave that boy or
the next
she ain't playing with these men
she owns all her own shit

no matter how bad it gets for your native auntie
she is strong
she holds her head up and can face her kids
knowing
she never had a moment of anger for them not once

your auntie teaches you the protocols for elders and Moon time
your auntie shows you how to smudge without saying a word
your auntie lays a feast out for the dead we miss
cuts hair when we mourn

your auntie paints polar bears and loons in acrylic on canvas
she sees it all different
your native auntie carries the teachings for the whole family
all the kids who don't care yet
but will

Finale

A friend vacuums up the pills off the floor

Unceasing tears flow
from faces you barely remember

A stranger who claims she's your mom asks
if you're okay

You choke on vomit while you hold a dead man's hand

Don't come in here if you're going to cry, his little boy says.

There are no words loud enough to drown out the voice of a
6-year-old girl
asking why her dad is white when he's supposed to be brown

He's white because he's dead, honey

My sadness is a lipstick stain –
use the right trick and it'll come right out
But you'll always see the little mark it left
And maybe wonder how it got there

Claim Laid

This is a prayer for the dead and dying –
and those that may never know a life on the outside

I hope your sins don't meet you at your grave –
grinning like a toothy menace –
I hope there's a twitch before they pounce

I hope your family knows it's okay to reconcile what you've done
with what you mean to them
But also okay not to –
if it gives them peace

I hope traffic and trains never rattle over your final resting place
to shake your bones to dust a little sooner

But most of all

I hope sagebrush bursts through your cedarwood coffin
and Eagle carries you home to Creator
I hope Thunderbird screams your name
and Coyote howls a lament for your spirit's journey

We will keep the fire burning for you

to light your way home

Acknowledgements

A version of "Finale" originally appeared in *Fevers of the Mind*,
Jun–Aug Issue, 2019

"My depression, my husband, and me" originally appeared in
Ayaskala online, 2019.

A version of "Thistle&Thorn" originally appeared in *Vaughn Street
Doubles*, Issue 4 online, 2020.

"That Boy" originally appeared in *Petrichor Journal* Issue 14 online,
2020.

Artwork on page 87 by Nixxi Knox.

Justene Dion-Glowa is a queer Métis creative, bead-worker and poet born in Win-Nipi (Winnipeg) and has been residing in Secwepemcúl'ecw since 2014. They are a Banff Centre for Arts and Creativity alumni. They have been working in the human services field for nearly a decade. Their microchap, *TEETH*, is available from Ghost City Press. *Trailer Park Shakes* is their first full-length poetry book.